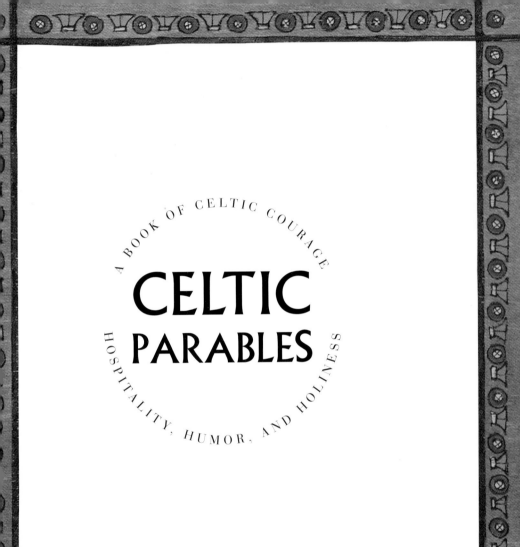

A BOOK OF CELTIC COURAGE

CELTIC
PARABLES

HOSPITALITY, HUMOR, AND HOLINESS

A BOOK OF CELTIC COURAGE

CELTIC

PARABLES

HOSPITALITY, HUMOR, AND HOLINESS

ROBERT VAN DE WEYER

ABINGDON PRESS
Nashville

Celtic Parables

Copyright © 1999 John Hunt Publishing

Text © 1999 Robert Van de Weyer

Abingdon Press edition published 1999

Picture research by Vanessa Fletcher
Illustrations by Katty McMurray

The publishers would like to thank the following for the use of pictures:
Bridgeman Art Library: p. 51 (St. Florentin, Nr. Auxerre, France)
Giles Conacher O.S.B. : p. 45
Fortean Picture Library: pp. 13 (Janet and Colin Ford), 41 (Janet and Colin Ford)
Images Library: p. 29

Designed by
THE BRIDGEWATER BOOK COMPANY LTD

ISBN 0-687-02911-2

Cataloging-in-Publication data is available from the Library of Congress

Original edition published in English under the title *Celtic Parables* by John Hunt
Publishing, Alresford, Hants, UK

99 00 01 02 03 04 05 06 -- 10 9 8 7 6 5 4 3 2 1

Manufactured in Singapore

INTRODUCTION:

THE STORIES OF THE CELTS *page 6*

THE STORIES OF THE CELTS

In common with most primitive peoples, the ancient Celts loved telling tales. On dark winter evenings around the hearth, old men and women related the stories which they themselves had heard from their parents and grandparents. And with each telling and re-telling, the stories were subtly altered, sometimes to add color and excitement, and sometimes to draw out the lessons which the children and young people should learn. In this way countless tales were passed down the generations from the earliest times. In the nineteenth century, when the old Celtic languages were being overwhelmed by English, there was a risk that many of these tales might be lost forever. Happily, however, many of the ancient stories were finally committed to paper during this period, and so have been preserved for future generations to enjoy.

The security of Celtic faith allowed them to question their God.

There are many tales of kings and their warriors, recalling their heroic exploits on the battlefield. There are tales of intrigue and treachery amongst men of wealth and power. And there are tales of love and romance. But the favorite tales of the Celts, especially after their conversion to Christianity, were religious. The modern mind may feel frustrated at the mixture of historical fact and myth in these spiritual stories; and scholars have tried to separate one from the other, with uncertain results. To the Celtic mind, however, only the inner truth mattered. Even when they were manifestly based on history, the stories were parables, filled with divine meaning.

Generally these religious tales concern a particular man or woman of great sanctity, and in some way reveal the qualities of holiness. One quality, which is frequently lauded, is moral courage, in which the saint upholds the truth against fierce opposition. Patrick, who is credited with converting Ireland to Christianity, and Iltut and David, who began the conversion of Ireland, are the most notable exemplars. A second quality is physical courage, exemplified by Brendan and his monks who sailed across the treacherous waters of the Atlantic Ocean in a coracle. A third quality is open hospitality, shown by Brigid. A fourth quality is self-deprecating humor, in which Columba and Aidan excelled. But

perhaps the most astonishing feature of holiness, in Celtic eyes, was the ability to relate to animals and to win their trust. Kevin, Piran, Cuthbert, Mungo, Colman, and Owen all display such qualities, each creating communities of creatures.

There is a second type of religious story beloved by the Celts, in which the hero is a sage, who conveys his wisdom with great wit. These stories are legion in number, and come from every part of the Celtic world. Sometimes the sage is named, and sometimes he remains anonymous. This volume contains a sample, and the hero is given the name of one of the great Irish sages, Comgan.

Like all good stories, the Celtic parables can be enjoyed simply as entertainment. But if their spiritual meaning is heeded, they are profoundly challenging, with disturbing lessons for the modern world.

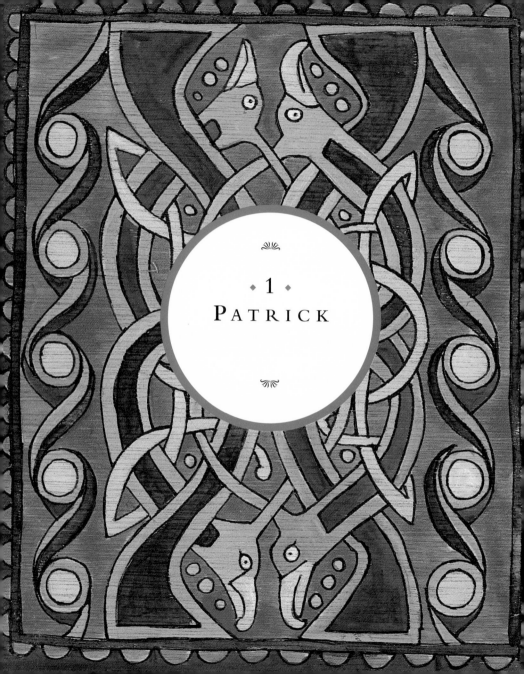

· 1 ·
PATRICK

SLAVERY

I, Patrick, am the most unlearned and the lowest of all the faithful. My father was a deacon, and my grandfather a priest. At the age of sixteen I was taken captive and shipped to Ireland, along with thousands of others.

When I arrived in Ireland, I was sent to tend sheep. I used to pray many times each day; and as I prayed, I felt God's love fill my heart and strengthen my faith. I had to stay all night in a hut on the mountain, looking after the sheep, and each day I would wake to pray before dawn in all weathers – snow, frost, and rain. I remained as a slave in Ireland for six years.

One night when I was asleep, I heard a voice speaking to me. It told me that a ship was waiting to take me home. I awoke, and immediately ran down the mountain, and hurried to the coast. I found a ship about to set sail; and although the captain did not want to take me, one of the old sailors smuggled me aboard.

I was overjoyed to see my family again, and at first thought I should never leave them again. But one night I had another dream in which a voice spoke to me. The voice implored me to return to Ireland, and preach the Gospel. When I awoke I felt as if I were a slave again – but now God was my master.

MISSION

When I arrived in Ireland, I decided
that I should preach the Gospel
initially to the kings and chieftains; and
once they had been converted, their
people would be eager to hear about
the new faith. Also I decided to use
one king to help convert another. Thus
when one king submitted to Christ, I
asked if he would allow me to take his
sons, carrying gifts to indicate good
will, to the next king.

By this means over a period of
thirty years I brought the Gospel to
every kingdom and every district of
Ireland. I baptized many thousands of
people. And I trained and ordained
numerous young men as priests. In the
course of my ministry I received many
gifts. But I never kept any of these gifts
for myself; instead I gave them as
presents to kings, and as ransoms for
the release of slaves.

At times I have encountered
hostility, and I and my companions
have spent many days and nights in
chains. But always we have won the
hearts of our captors, so they released
us and embraced the Gospel.

ACCUSATIONS

Now that Christianity has become the
main religion of Ireland, some ambitious
and greedy priests have made false
accusations against me, saying that I have
accumulated great wealth by demanding
gifts. They hope to discredit me, and
assume control of the Church in Ireland.

I acknowledge that in this present
world I am exalted above my true merit,
and I am more privileged than I deserve.
I am more suited to poverty and adversity
than to riches and luxury – for the Lord
Christ was poor for our sakes. Yet in truth
I have no wealth of my own. And I have
no desire for wealth. On the contrary I
am willing to be killed or reduced once
more to slavery, for the sake of the Gospel.

I now commend my soul to God, for
whom, despite my obscurity, I have
served as ambassador. Indeed, in choosing
such a lowly person as me for this noble
task, God has shown that He is no
respecter of persons. May God never
separate me from His people on this
island, which stands at the very edge of
the Earth. And may God always make me
a faithful witness of His saving love, until
He calls me to heaven.

*St. Patrick returned to Ireland, where he had been a slave for
six years, to bring the Gospel to every kingdom.*

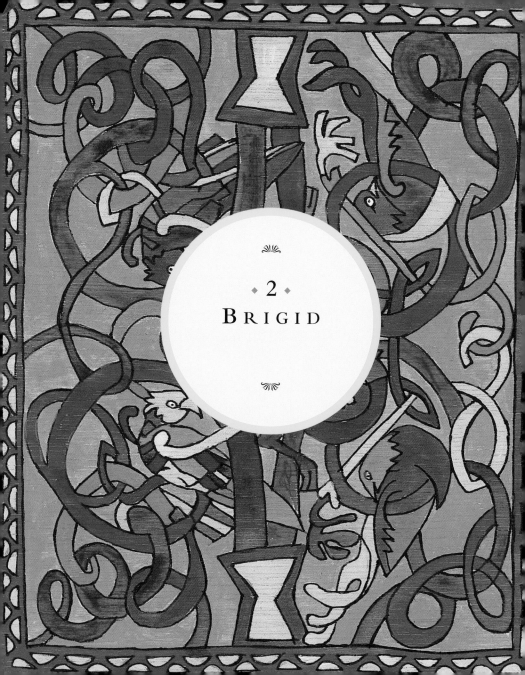

· 2 ·

BRIGID

THE SWORD AND THE LEPER

Brigid's father was a wealthy chieftain, living in a large, luxurious castle; and in its cellar was a vast larder filled with fine food. Each day the young Brigid took from the larder as much food as she could carry, and gave it to the poor and the sick. This generosity angered her father; and eventually he decided to try and sell her as a slave. So he grabbed her by the arm, and threw her into his chariot. He then rode toward the castle of a neighboring chieftain.

When they arrived at the castle gate, Brigid's father unbuckled his sword, as a sign that he came in peace, and he left the sword in the chariot. He then entered the castle, leaving Brigid outside. A few minutes later a leper appeared, and begged Brigid to help him. She gave him her father's sword.

In the meantime her father was negotiating a price for her, persuading the other chieftain that she was a diligent and honest worker. Eventually the two men reached an agreement, and emerged from the castle. When her father saw that his sword was missing, he knew at once that Brigid had given it away. Immediately he flew into a rage, and in his wrath he started to beat her. The other chieftain intervened, and asked Brigid why she had stolen her father's property. Brigid replied: "If I had the power, I should take all his wealth and your wealth, and give it to Christ's brothers and sisters — to whom it really belongs."

The chieftain laughed, and said to Brigid's father: "I am afraid your daughter is too honest for me. You'll have to keep her." So by her own kindness Brigid was saved from slavery.

THE CROSS OF RUSHES

As a young woman Brigid decided to become a hermit; and she built a hut for herself under a large oak tree. Soon large numbers of both women and men came to join, to live as nuns and monks; and within a few years Brigid's monastery had grown larger than any town in the land.

Every evening after dusk the nuns and monks, led by Brigid, searched the lanes and ditches in the surrounding area, looking for those with no place to rest. They brought them back to the monastery, where they gave them a meal and a bed. Brigid also ran a huge hospital, where the nuns and monks nursed sick people from throughout the country.

Near the monastery was a large house where a wealthy merchant lived. He disliked religion, and openly expressed his contempt for Brigid's monastery. Nonetheless she regularly visited him, and he could not help admiring the strength of her convictions. The merchant caught a fatal illness; and as he lay on his death-bed, he sent for Brigid.

By the time Brigid arrived the dying merchant could not speak. Brigid knew that no words could comfort him. So she reached down to the floor, where fresh rushes had been laid. She took a bundle of rushes, tied them into a simple cross, and placed the cross in the merchant's hands. He lifted the cross to his lips, and kissed it.

A few moments later he was dead.

Saved from slavery, St. Brigid was to found a monastery and tend the sick.

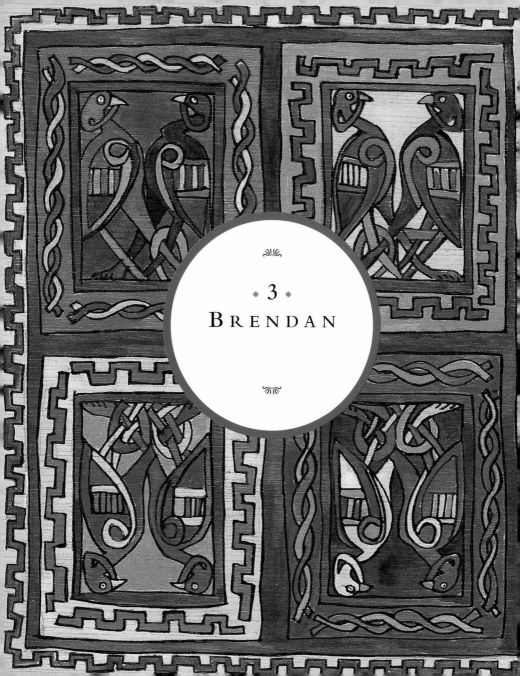

· 3 ·

BRENDAN

THE FAROES

All true Celts yearned to be pilgrims, allowing God to guide them to foreign lands. And the most famous Celtic pilgrim was Brendan.

Brendan was the abbot of a large monastery. One February he left the monastery, and spent the season of Lent on a high mountain overlooking the Atlantic Ocean. As he stared at the sea, he conceived the idea of sailing across it. At Easter he returned to his monastery and asked for monks to accompany him. Twelve monks came forward.

Brendan led the twelve monks to the coast, and there they made a coracle. The ribs and frame were carved out of oak, and then covered with oxhide tanned in oak bark. They smeared the seams with grease to make them waterproof, storing extra hides and grease for repairs. They erected a mast and attached a simple sail. And they loaded food for forty days, allowing themselves only enough to eat every third day. They pushed the boat down the beach into the water and clambered aboard.

They trusted God to send winds and currents that would take them to wherever he wanted. After forty days they arrived at the largest of the Faroe Islands. There they found a hermit who had come by coracle many years earlier. The hermit was delighted to see Brendan and his brethren, and invited them to celebrate Easter with him.

At their Easter service thousands of birds, all with pure white plumage, perched on the surrounding trees; and as the monks chanted the Easter anthems, the birds sang also, and flapped their wings in perfect rhythm.

ICELAND

At the end of the Easter season Brendan and his monks once more set sail. The winds and currents took the coracle into colder waters. One day they saw a vast column rising from the sea. They were utterly mystified by this strange object; it shone like silver, it was as clear as crystal, and as hard as marble. The coracle drifted toward the column. The monks look down into the water, and could see that the column was as deep as it was high.

And when they touched it, they realized it was made of ice. Then the sun appeared from behind clouds, and shone through the column to give a dazzling white light.

Eight days later the monks reached a vast rocky island that was bare of grass and trees. As they drew closer they heard a noise like the blowing of bellows, followed by the din of a hammer on an anvil; and they could see smoke rising from behind the rocks. The monks trembled with fear and prayed for protection. Then a crowd of men, their faces dark and grimy, came down to the sea, each carrying a huge piece of blazing rock in a pair of tongs. They threw the rocks at the monks. None reached the coracle; and as the rocks hit the water, they sent up a thick cloud of steam.

At that moment the wind changed, pushing the coracle away from the island. The monks were relieved to escape. But Brendan was sad, because he could not preach the Gospel to these men. He prayed that at some time in the future the people of the island would welcome a Christian preacher and be converted by his words.

NEWFOUNDLAND

After many days Brendan and his monks saw land. The winds and currents brought them to a small creek, just wide enough for the prow of the coracle. Brendan jumped onto the rocks, and climbed up the cliff. At the top were two caves facing each other. In the mouth of one cave a tiny spring gushed forth; and inside the other cave was a hermit – who, like the hermit in the Faroes, had sailed here many years earlier.

The hermit came out to greet Brendan, embracing him warmly. When the other monks appeared, he embraced them all with the same warmth, calling each by their names. They asked him how he knew their names. He smiled, and said: "I have spent many years in contemplation."

The hermit introduced himself as Paul. Brendan asked him what food he ate. Paul replied: "When I arrived here thirty years ago, I crouched on the rocks by the sea, and tried to catch fish with my hands; but I could catch nothing. Then a seal emerged from the waves with a fish in its mouth, and laid it at my feet. And since that time a seal has appeared each day with a fish for me to eat."

Paul led Brendan and his monks down the cliff to the sea. And at that moment fourteen seals appeared, each with a fish in its mouth which it laid on the rocks. Then the fourteen pilgrims ate together.

Brendan and his monks stayed with Paul for many days. Finally Paul told them it was time to depart. For several hours seals appeared one by one, and put fish in the coracle to provide food for the journey.

THE AZORES

For forty days the coracle was blown back across the ocean into warmer waters. On the fortieth day a thick fog descended on the coracle, so Brendan and the monks could see nothing. When the fog lifted, they discovered they had landed on a sandy beach. The sun shone brilliantly, and in front of them lay a vast and bountiful orchard, its trees laden with huge fruit. The pilgrims thanked God for His mercy and ate their fill.

The following day they found a green, fertile country, watered by streams of pure, sparkling water. A handsome young man appeared, who, like Paul, knew their names. "Welcome," he exclaimed, "you have reached an earthly Paradise – a foretaste of the eternal Paradise which all virtuous people will enjoy. But you cannot stay here. Instead you must return home, to describe this island to others; and you must promise them that, if they follow God's commandments, they will inhabit an even lovelier realm. As proof of your visit you must each pick up twelve stones from the ground, and take them home." The monks bent down, and saw that every stone was a precious jewel.

The young man led them back to the coast. They put the jewels in the coracle, as well as fruit for the journey. It was so heavily laden it could barely float. But the wind was gentle and the waves low so they arrived home safely.

They told their story to all who would listen, and it circulated throughout the Christian world. And from that time onward it has inspired people to be virtuous – and brave.

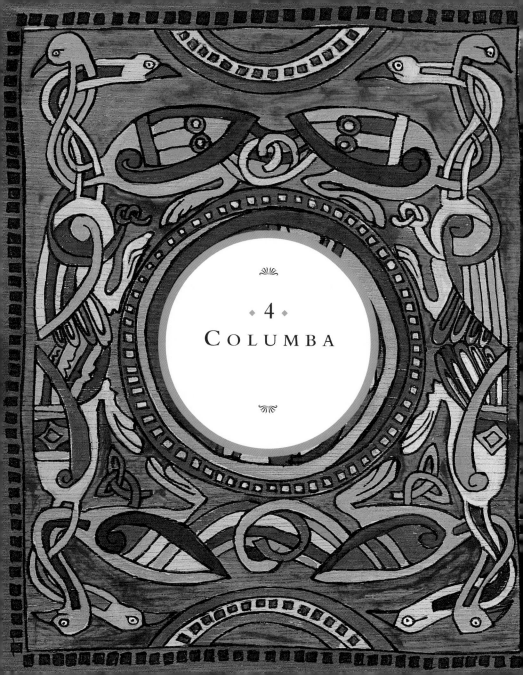

· 4 ·

COLUMBA

COLUMBA

As a young man Columba became a bard, composing songs that told the story of Jesus Christ; and he walked around Ireland singing these songs to the common people. Then he conceived the idea of establishing a network of communities, dedicated to composing and performing Christian music, and to educating young people. To obtain funds for these communities he visited kings and chieftains, winning their friendship and persuading them to make handsome donations.

The most famous of his communities were those at Derry and Kells. In addition to music, the monks also copied out the Gospels, decorating them with beautiful illustrations.

Sadly, in gaining the support of one king, Columba would earn the distrust of that king's enemies. Thus he became a controversial figure. In 563 he found himself on the losing side of one of the bloodiest battles in Irish history; and he was sentenced never to set foot again on Irish soil. He and twelve companions sailed near Derry to the west of Scotland, and they landed on a tiny island.

IONA

Enchanted by the remoteness and beauty of Iona, Columba decided to settle on the island, building a monastery there. He then made a succession of tours in the Scottish mainland, preaching the Gospel and winning converts. He invited the young male converts to his island to train as monks. He then sent them on preaching tours; and they recruited more young men as monks. By this means almost the whole of Scotland heard the Gospel, and the monastery grew very large. The island became known as Iona – the island of saints.

His success in winning converts to Christianity incurred the wrath of many pagan priests. On one occasion, when Columba arrived at Inverness, the local priests ordered that the gates of the city be closed to him. But he pointed to the gates, and slowly they swung open. In later years it was debated whether this was truly a miracle, or whether supporters in the city pulled the gates open. But the event so impressed the common people, that they embraced the Gospel.

TESTING A VOCATION

In central Scotland Columba converted a young farm laborer called Molluch. Although the young man could not read or write, he wanted Columba to ordain him as a priest.

"If I were a priest," Molluch said, "I would be able to care for the other Christians in this area, and I could also win new converts."

Columba decided to test Molluch's vocation. He took Molluch to a nearby lake, and found a coracle. "Go out in this coracle," Columba said, "and try to catch fish." Molluch was mystified, but did as Columba instructed. For two days and nights Molluch sat in the coracle, holding a rod over the side, but caught nothing. Then at dawn on the the third day, a fish bit on the hook, and Molluch hauled the fish aboard. But as soon as Molluch saw the fish with the hook in its mouth, he took pity. Carefully he extracted the hook, and threw the fish back into the water. Then he rowed back to the shore.

When he had explained to Columba what had happened, Columba smiled, and said: "You have proved that you have the three qualities necessary for the priesthood. First, you are patient. If you are willing to wait two days and two nights to catch a fish, you will wait two years, even two decades, to catch a soul. Secondly, you are compassionate. If you can take pity on a fish, then you show far greater pity for humans in need. Thirdly, you are humble. Even though you were the cause of the fish's distress, pride did not prevent you from saving it."

So Columba ordained Molluch, who proved an excellent priest.

NETTLE SOUP

One day, when he was visiting Iona's graveyard, Columba saw an old woman cutting nettles. He asked her why she was doing this. "Dear father," she replied, "I have no milk to drink, because my cow has not yet calved. So I am living on nettle soup." As he walked on, Columba thought: "If that woman eats only nettles in expectation of a calf, I should eat only nettles in expectation of God's kingdom." So he ordered the monastery cook to give him only nettle soup.

The cook was worried that such a meager diet would kill their beloved abbot. He made a special stick, hollow in the middle, for stirring the soup; and through this stick he secretly poured milk. So, far from becoming ill, Columba thrived on the soup; and soon he was urging the other monks to follow his example.

The cook now had to prepare a vast cauldron of nettle soup, pouring gallons of milk through the stick. Within a few days the monastery had run out of milk, and the cook had to confess his deception. For a moment Columba's face went red with anger. Then he burst into laughter, saying: "It is God's joke against me. It was pride that made me tell others of my diet – so I deserve to be tricked."

From then onward he ordered that all the monks on Iona should eat proper, nutritious meals.

Turfs as shoes

After Columba had been on Iona many years, he received a message from Ireland, saying that the senior bishop there had decided to outlaw the traveling bards. Remembering how successful he had been in winning converts through his songs; he decided to sail to Ireland, to try and overturn the bishop's decision.

In addition to food for the journey, he stored in the boat two large turfs which he had dug from the Iona soil. When he landed on the Irish coast, he tied the turfs to his feet – so he would abide by the sentence never to set foot again on Irish soil.

He walked on these turfs toward Armagh, where the senior bishop lived. As he walked he sang his old songs. People ran from the fields and poured out of their homes to hear him; and many of them followed him. When he arrived at the bishop's house, he was leading a huge crowd. The bishop told Columba that he disliked the bards because they conveyed the Gospel in their own words, rather than in words they had been taught by bishops and priests. Columba replied that they sang from the heart, so their words were sent by God's Spirit. The bishop was frightened by the size of the crowd and relented, agreeing to rescind his order and let Columba carry on his work.

The White Horse

In early May in 597 Columba, weary with age, was taken on a wagon around Iona. Wherever he saw monks working in the fields, he stood up and blessed them. Wherever he saw cattle and sheep grazing in the fields, he stood up and blessed them. And he also blessed the wild animals as they scampered past, and the birds as they flew overhead. He went to the monastery's barns, and was pleased to see them full, saying: "If I have to depart from my family, I shall carry with me the knowledge that they have ample food for the coming year."

Near the granary he climbed down from the wagon, and sat on a rock. The white horse which had been pulling the wagon came to Columba. It laid its head on Columba's breast, and began to whinny, and then to weep and foam at the mouth. It seemed to know that its master was about to die. Another monk tried to push the horse away, but Columba forbade him, saying: "Let him alone, for he loves me. Let him pour his tears of grief onto my bosom. You, a man with a rational soul, can know nothing about my departure except what I tell you. But this dumb creature, possessing no reason, has been told by the Creator Himself that I am about to leave him."

Elated by what he had seen, Columba then climbed a small hill overlooking the monastery. He raised both arms and blessed the monastery, saying: "On this place, small and poor as it is, the kings of the people of these lands will bestow great honor."

COLUMBA'S DEATH

Columba returned to his cell, where he spent the night sitting up on the bare stone which served as his bed. He dictated his last command to his monks: "Be at peace with one another. So long as you are at peace, the Lord will bless you and all your work." He then fell silent.

When the church bell tolled for midnight prayers, he rose up and hastened toward the church, arriving first. He went up to the altar and knelt down. As the other monks entered, they were astonished to see the whole church bathed in a soft, golden light, which emanated from the altar.

As the monks reached the altar Columba was overcome and collapsed. One of the monks laid Columba's head on his lap. Columba opened his eyes and looked round him. He saw all his monks weeping. His face broke into a joyful smile, and with a great effort he lifted his right hand in order to bless them. Their tears stopped, and they too smiled with joy, knowing that their beloved father would soon receive his eternal reward.

Columba's hand then fell back onto his breast. His face now started to glow with joy, as he saw the angels coming to receive him into heaven. Then, filled with contentment, he breathed his last.

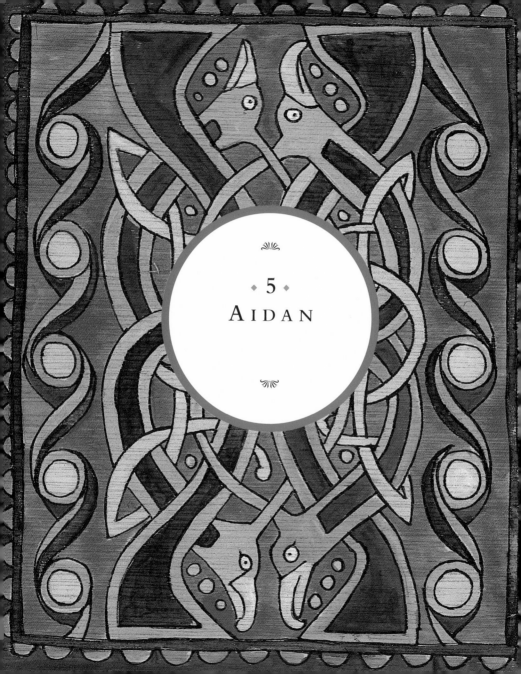

· 5 ·
AIDAN

Spiritual Milk and Meat

King Oswald of Northumbria, who had heard of the blessings enjoyed by converts to Christianity, asked the monks of Iona to send a bishop to his kingdom, to teach himself and his people. They first sent a man of the most austere disposition, who antagonized the people of Northumbria. He soon returned to Iona, reporting to his brethren that the Northumbrians were too obstinate and barbarous to receive the Gospel. The abbot called a meeting of the monks to discuss what should be done. A young monk called Aidan said to the brother who had been to Northumbria: "It seems to me you were too severe with your ignorant hearers. Follow the example of the apostles, who began by giving the people the milk of simple teaching, gradually nourishing them until they were capable of digesting strong spiritual meat."

The other monks realized at once that Aidan was the right man to send as bishop to Northumbria; he was endowed with the gift of discretion, the most precious gift for a teacher.

When Aidan arrived in Northumbria, he was greeted warmly by King Oswald, who gave him the island of Lindisfarne on which to build a monastery. The king's castle at Bamburgh stood on a cliff overlooking Lindisfarne; and at low tide it was possible to walk across the sands between the two.

Mission to All

Aidan won numerous converts in Northumbria by the sweetness of his words and by the holiness of his life. He neither sought nor cared for any worldly possessions. He refused to travel on horseback, but always traveled on foot, so he could meet the common people. As he walked he spoke to everyone he passed, both rich and poor, telling them about Jesus Christ. If they embraced the faith, he baptized them in the nearest stream.

He was indifferent to people's wealth or status. If a rich or powerful person did wrong, he spoke to them frankly, urging them to repent; and he was equally frank with the poor and humble. He soon won the respect of the entire population. Many rich people offered gifts, which he received gratefully. But he never kept the gifts for himself; instead he passed them to the poor, or used them to ransom slaves. Many of the ransomed slaves became Christians, and some he trained as monks and preachers at Lindisfarne.

THE SILVER DISH

One Easter King Oswald invited Aidan to dine with him. A lavish meal was brought to them. Aidan had raised his hand to bless the food, when a servant came in to tell the king that a great crowd of needy people had assembled outside the castle, begging for alms. Oswald immediately ordered the food to be given to them; he then broke the dish with his hands, and distributed the pieces among them. Aidan was so moved at such generosity that he took hold of the king's hands, and exclaimed: "May these hands never wither." Later events proved that this prayer was heard: when Oswald was killed in battle, his hands were cut off from his body, and they did not decay.

THE FINE HORSE

When Aidan was growing old, King Oswald gave him a very fine horse, to spare his spindly legs and help him continue to carry out his good work in comfort. Soon afterward, when Aidan was traveling through the countryside, he met a poor man who begged him for help. Aidan immediately dismounted, and, overcome with feelings of pity and charity, gave the beggar his horse.

When King Oswald heard about Aidan's action, he felt angry and hurt. When he next saw Aidan, he said: "You should not have given away such a fine horse, which I had specially selected for you. I have many less valuable horses that are good enough for the poor." Aidan exclaimed: "What are you saying? Is that horse more important to you than the child of God to whom I gave it?" The king paused for a moment. Then he unbuckled his sword, throwing it aside, and knelt at Aidan's feet. "I beg your forgiveness," he cried; "I shall never again question what you do with my gifts." Aidan was deeply moved, and blessed the king.

St. Aidan, who left Iona to convert the people of Northumbria to Christianity.

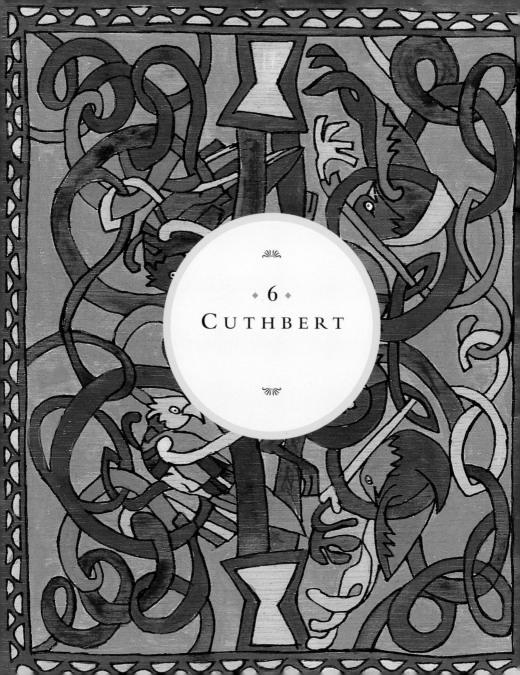

· 6 ·

CUTHBERT

BOYHOOD

As a boy Cuthbert was interested only in sports. He was agile, strong, and quick-witted, so he excelled at every sport he played. At the age of eight he boasted that he had beaten boys of twice his age at wrestling, running, and jumping.

One day he was playing in a field with a large crowd of other boys, when a child, seemingly no more than three years old, ran up to him. The little boy spoke with the gravity of a man, scolding him for wasting his time on idle games, instead of training his mind and body to serve God. Cuthbert burst out in mocking laughter, and the boy burst into tears. Cuthbert tried to console him, but the boy stared him in the eye, and said: "You are a stubborn fool." The words went straight to Cuthbert's heart, and the smile faded from his face. He embraced the boy, thanking him for his boldness, and the boy instantly stopped weeping.

Cuthbert gave up all sport, and went to work as a shepherd in the hills above Melrose. There he spent many hours of each day praying and studying the Bible. One night he was looking eastward to the coast, and he saw a shaft of light rising up into the darkness. The next day he learned that at that very moment Aidan had died. He became convinced that the light was a sign from God, calling him to be Aidan's successor.

Cuthbert ran down to the monastery at Melrose, and asked to become a monk. He soon gained the respect of his brethren, who admired his hard manual work in the monastery garden, as well as his spiritual devotion.

He traveled frequently to nearby homesteads, to strengthen people's faith. At one time a plague raged through the neighborhood, prompting many to abandon Christianity, and revert to pagan magic. Cuthbert walked tirelessly across the hills, trying to rescue people from their errors. His gentleness of manner, together with his skill in making the mysteries of faith plain and simple, won the hearts of all whom he met.

In order to devote more time to prayer, and to harden his body, he used to rise in the middle of the night, and walk down to the nearby river. He would wade in and sing hymns. Then he would climb back onto the bank, and recite psalms. Two otters would rise out of the water, and lie beside him; the warmth of their breath and their bodies would dry him.

After many years at Melrose, Cuthbert was invited to go to Lindisfarne as abbot. Cuthbert was overjoyed, because this was the fulfillment of his boyhood vision – that he would become Aidan's successor.

He was appalled to find that the monastery at Lindisfarne had grown very slack since Aidan's death. Austerity and spiritual devotion had become superseded by idleness and relaxation. The monks were eating rich food and employing servants, and their worship was brief and perfunctory. When Cuthbert chastised them, the monks hurled insults at him. But he refused to be provoked, and always responded with kind words. And though the laxness grieved him, he remained outwardly cheerful. He worked hard, assisting the servants: he dug the monastery garden, cooked meals, and cleaned the floors. He also remained in church after the worship had finished, to say his private prayers. Even the most corrupt monks were impressed by his example, and one by one the monks began to imitate him.

Eventually Cuthbert became weary of his reponsibilities at Lindisfarne, and yearned to live alone as a hermit. So he sailed to Farne Island, a rocky outcrop several miles out to sea. Using rough stone he built a small hut for himself, a chapel, and a guest house.

At first he depended on bread brought by visitors. But he wanted to grow his own food, so he dug a patch of ground and planted wheat. By midsummer the wheat had not sprouted, so he planted barley instead. This grew and ripened. But as he was about to harvest it, a flock of birds flew down to devour it. Cuthbert called out: "Why are you eating crops you did not sow? Is your need greater than mine?" The birds flew off, and Cuthbert harvested the barley.

Some time later the birds returned, and began taking the thatch from the guest house to build their nests. He called out to them, and they flew away.

Three days later one of the birds returned, and landed in front of Cuthbert. The bird's feathers were ruffled, and his head was drooping, as if begging forgiveness. Cuthbert was delighted, and forgave all the birds immediately. Shouting at the top of his voice, he invited the birds to return to the island. The flock swooped down, carrying lumps of pigs' lard. Cuthbert kept the lard in the guest house, and polished visitors' shoes with it, saying to them: "If birds can show humility, so should we."

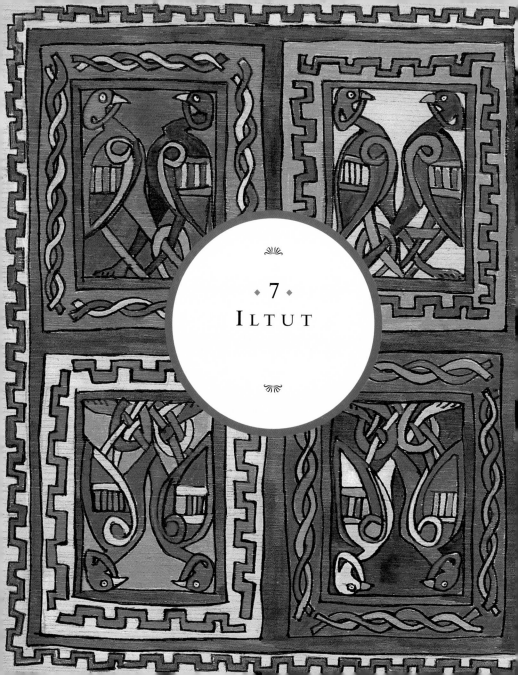

· 7 ·

ILTUT

CONVERSION

As a young man Iltut dreamed only of fighting glorious battle. He joined the army of King Paulinus of Glamorgan in Wales. The young soldier so impressed the king with his bravery and prowess that he promoted him to the highest rank – and he invited Iltut to reside at his castle.

One day Iltut took a group of knights hunting, going to a remote forest where a hermit called Cadoc lived. Iltut became separated from the other knights, who came across Cadoc's hut. They demanded food and drink, threatening to kill Cadoc if he did not comply. Cadoc invited them in, and served them with all the food he had. The knights treated Cadoc like a slave; and they told obscene jokes in the hope of provoking Cadoc to anger. But Cadoc simply smiled at their folly.

Iltut eventually arrived at the hut, and was horrified to observe the knights' behavior. He ordered the knights to leave, and then dropped down on his knees, begging forgiveness for them. Cadoc lifted Iltut to his feet and warmly embraced him.

That night Iltut lay awake in bed, his heart filled with love and admiration for Cadoc. "This man," Iltut thought, "is a far braver soldier than I am. I fight human foes, but he is fighting the Devil. I have a sword and lance, but he has only prayer. Yet I can only win a few battles, while he can win ultimate victory." Just before dawn Iltut put on a rough woollen cloak and slipped out of the royal castle, to spend the rest of his life making war against the Devil.

FIRST HERMITAGE

Iltut walked southward to the coast, and came to a wide valley, with steep cliffs on either side, running down to the beach. Iltut built himself a hut in the valley, and spent the following three months learning how to pray.

One day a stag galloped down the valley, and bounded into Iltut's hut. A few moments later a pack of hounds arrived, barking wildly. As soon as they reached the hut the hounds fell silent, and stood quite still with their heads bowed. Finally King Paulinus with a group of knights rode up, and ordered the hounds to go into the hut; but the hounds remained motionless.

Then Iltut emerged from the hut, and welcomed the king and the knights. They were so astonished to see him that for a moment they were speechless. Then the king erupted, his face ablaze with anger, accusing Iltut of betraying him. Iltut smiled; and when the king had finished shouting, he invited him and the knights into his hut for a meal. At that moment the stag poked his head out of the hut, and looked plaintively at the king.

The king's temper immediately cooled, and he accepted Iltut's invitation. Over the meal Iltut told the story of his conversion, and explained that he now lived in harmony with all God's creatures – such as the stag who trusted him, and the hounds who bowed before him.

SCHOOL

As King Paulinus listened to Iltut, his heart melted, and he too embraced Christianity. He asked whether he could send his son to Iltut to be educated. Iltut was delighted to accept the boy, and immediately built a hut for him. Soon noblemen and merchants followed the example of the king, begging Iltut to educate their sons. Iltut accepted them all, and soon his valley was filled with huts – he had unwittingly founded the largest school in Britain.

Through reading the Bible Iltut had come to believe in the equal value of all labor, intellectual and manual, and in the equal value of all people. So he invited the sons of farmers and craftsmen to join his school. And all the pupils spent each morning on intellectual studies, and each afternoon growing and cooking their own food. In this way all divisions of class and work were broken down.

SECOND HERMITAGE

After many years running his school, Iltut felt weary. He decided to move to some remote spot, and devote the remainder of his life to solitary prayer, preparing himself for death. But he knew that if he announced this intention publicly, people would follow him to discover his new home; he would then be constantly interrupted by visitors seeking his advice.

So just as he had once slipped out of the royal castle under cover of darkness, he now left his school in the middle of a moonless night. He walked westward along the coast, until he reached a beautiful golden beach at the end of a long peninsula. Beside the beach was a cave, which Iltut made his home. A flat rock served as his bed, and the seagulls were his companions. He allowed his hair and beard to grow long, in the hope that passing travelers would not recognize him and he would at last gain peace.

For many weeks pupils and teachers from his school scoured the countryside of south Wales in search of him; but eventually they gave up in despair. Then a year later one of his pupils, called David, happened to be walking along the coast, and noticed Iltut trying to catch fish with a net. He walked over to him, and prostrated himself at his feet. Iltut lifted him to his feet, and embraced him. David then continued his journey, without speaking a word – he understood his former master's desire for solitude.

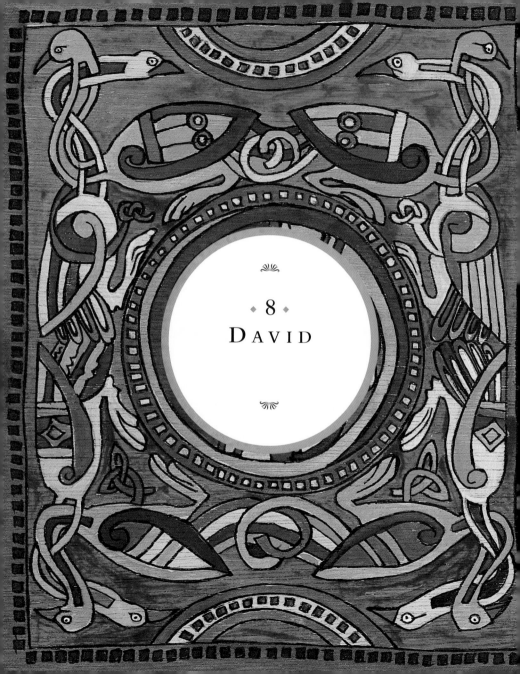

· 8 ·

DAVID

COMMISSION

David remained at Iltut's school for several more years, becoming one of the senior teachers. Then one day he decided to visit Iltut again in his cave. When he arrived Iltut was lying on his stone bed, breathing heavily.

Iltut beckoned David to come close, and whispered to him: "Soon I shall be dead. When I have died, do not conduct any kind of funeral; simply put stones at the mouth of the cave, so my home becomes my tomb. As for you, do not return to my school, which is for all kinds of young people. You are called to be a preacher, and you must start a school for other preachers. Continue westward, until you can go no further. Find a sheltered place suitable for a school, and then go out preaching the Gospel. When young men convert to Christianity, invite them back to your school to train as preachers – and then send them out to recruit more preachers. By this means you will bring Christianity to the whole country."

When Iltut died, David closed the cave with stones, and walked to the southwest tip of Wales.

PREACHING

David settled in a valley near a beach, similar to the valley where Iltut's school was situated. He built himself a hut, and then went out preaching. He found that he could explain the Gospel with great eloquence, in a manner which the common people could understand. In each place he visited, his good nature and the spiritual example he set won him many converts.

He did not try to refute or destroy the traditional religion in these places, but taught that Christianity was the fulfillment of that religion, making plain its inner truths. He urged his converts to continue worshiping at their traditional shrines, but to use Christian prayers and hymns.

He stayed in each place several weeks, guiding the people in their new faith. During this time he discerned which young men had a gift for speaking. He then took these young men back to his school, and trained them – as Iltut had instructed. In this way he established a vast team of preachers, who gradually spread across the whole of Wales.

TRAINING

David's school for preachers was visible from the sea. One day, when David was away, a band of pirates saw and attacked it; they seized all the young men and took them to Ireland to sell as slaves.

When he returned and learned what had happened, David looked for a place that could not be seen from the sea. Eventually he found a hollow, which was covered in yellow flowers. He took the flowers as a sign from God that this was the right location. He soon recruited new members, and the school again flourished. The yellow flowers became known as daffodils –

after the Welsh form of David's name. And a church was built with a high tower; but the hollow was so deep, that the tower was invisible to outsiders.

As David's reputation grew, young men began to arrive at the school without invitation, asking to join the community. To test their calling, David left these men at the school gate for ten days; and the existing members pretended to be hostile, making rude and abusive remarks. If the men remained at the gate, it demonstrated that they were convinced of their calling – and that they could endure the insults which preachers by their nature must endure.

St. David, who traveled to Wales to establish a school for preachers.

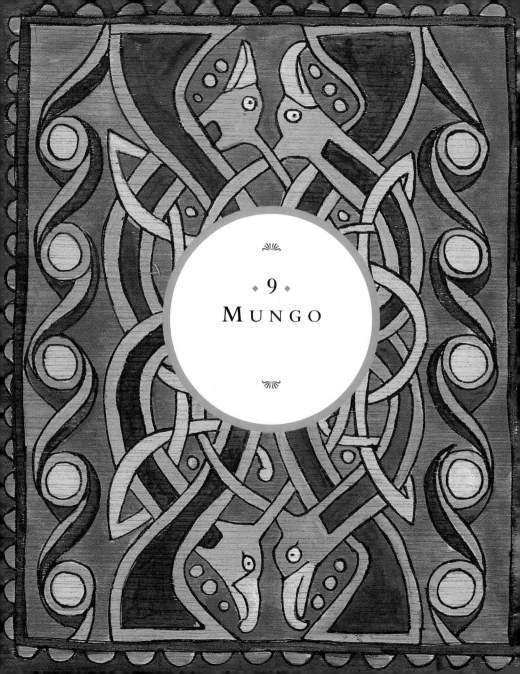

· 9 ·

MUNGO

FINDING THE SITE

Mungo believed that God was calling him to found a new monastery amidst the tribesmen of central Scotland. So he set out from home in search of a suitable place.

Soon a wild hound appeared, and began to lead him. The hound took him over steep mountains, into deep valleys, and through dark forests. Each night Mungo and the hound lay down in the grass next to each other; and before they fell asleep they talked to each other, Mungo speaking in words, and the hound replying with barks and growls.

Eventually they arrived in a beautiful lush valley, with a clear blue river running through it. Around the valley they could see little columns of smoke, so they knew there were many tribal people living there. The hound stopped near the river bank, and began scratching the ground with its paws, tearing up tufts of grass. Mungo fell to his knees, asking God whether this was truly the place to build his monastery.

At that moment a little robin flew down from a tree, landing on Mungo's shoulder. It flapped its wings, and kissed Mungo on the cheek with its beak. Mungo knew that, if even the birds welcomed him in this way, this was the perfect place to found his monastery. The hound went off to collect branches, and the bird collected leaves and grass; and with these materials Mungo was able to build himself a hut.

Then the hound came up to Mungo and growled loudly, bowing its head. Mungo laid his hand on its head, and blessed it, praying for God's guidance on it. The hound then bounded off, and in the following days and months sent other men to Mungo, all of whom had also felt called to start a new monastery. The robin and the hound collected materials for each one to build himself a hut.

As the monastery grew, the local people came to visit it, wanting to see their new neighbors. Mungo did not at first speak about their faith, but invited the people to bring the sick to the monastery, saying that he and his brethren would nurse and try to heal them. The people could not understand why these young men were making this offer; but the young men were manifestly sincere, so the people brought their sick to them. Through loving care, and the use of local herbs as medicines, Mungo and his brethren healed many of them. Where the illness was terminal, Mungo and his brethren found herbs that eased the physical pain – and they gave unstinting love, which eased the spiritual pain.

Soon people were asking Mungo about the religion which inspired them. Only then did Mungo speak about his faith. Within a few years the whole valley was Christian, and the people built a large church near the monastery – the forerunner of Glasgow cathedral.

St. Mungo inspired the people of Scotland to convert to Christianity after demonstrating his skills as a healer.

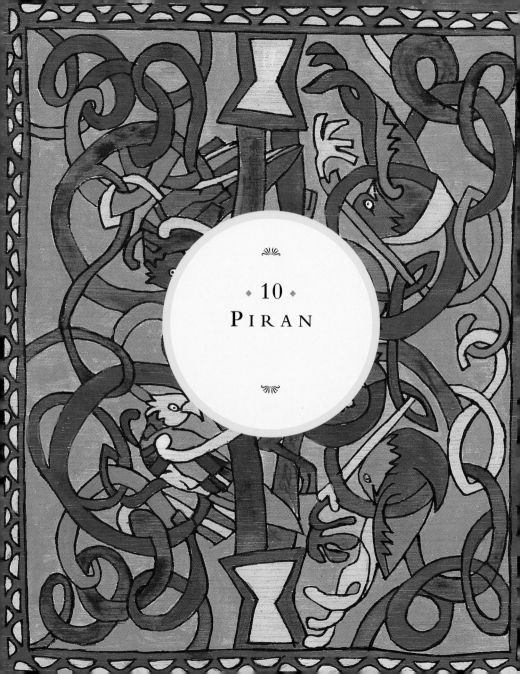

10
PIRAN

THE ANIMAL MONASTERY

Piran was a monk at the monastery where Brendan lived. Like Brendan he felt called to put to sea. But, whereas Brendan took companions, Piran wanted to go alone; and whereas Brendan set sail from the west coast of Ireland, Piran was drawn to the east. So he walked eastward to the sea, and built himself a coracle. The winds and the currents took him to Cornwall, where he landed on a sandy beach.

He walked across the beach, and sat down under a tree. Sitting under the same tree was a wild boar. On seeing Piran, the boar fled in terror. But then, sensing Piran's love for all creatures, the boar returned, and sat beside Piran. After a while Piran ordered the boar to tear branches and grass with its teeth, and bring them to him. Piran used them to build two huts, one for himself and the other for the boar. Thus the boar became Piran's first monk.

Soon other animals came out of the forest to join Piran and the boar: a fox, a badger, a wolf, and a doe. Together they formed a community, each collecting food for all to share.

THE FOX'S THEFT

One night the fox crept into Piran's hut, and stole his leather shoes. Abandoning his intention to live as a monk, he carried the shoes to his old lair in the forest, and chewed them there. When he realized what had happened, Piran sent the badger after the fox, to persuade him to return to the monastery. So the badger, who knew the forest well, went straight to the fox's lair; and, seeing the fox about to eat Piran's shoes, bit his ears and tail. Then, with his teeth in the fox's fur, he dragged him back to the monastery.

Piran asked the fox: "Why did you commit this crime, dear brother?" "Master," the fox replied, "I craved the taste of meat. I could not bear to live only on the nuts and berries and roots which the others bring." Piran said: "I understand your craving, because you have always eaten meat. And I admire you for wanting to chew my shoes, which have the taste of meat, rather than killing another animal for its flesh."

From then onward Piran himself went into the forest each day, to look for small animals which had died naturally, bringing them back for the fox to enjoy.

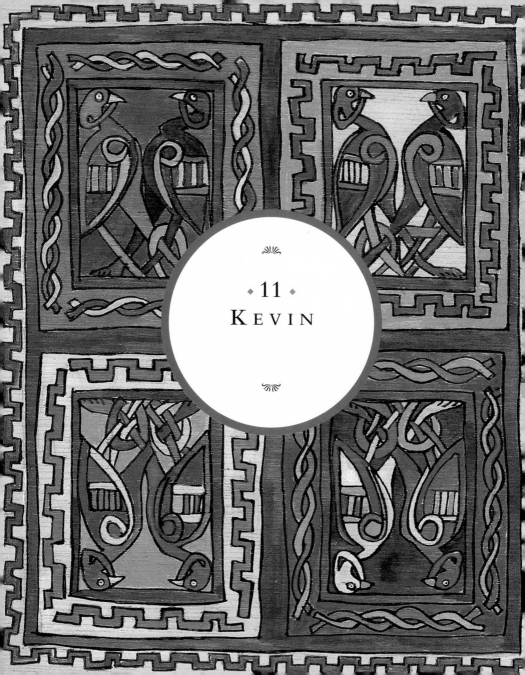

· 11 ·

KEVIN

THE COW

Kevin went to live as a hermit on the banks of a small lake, near the top of a mountain. He gathered herbs to eat, and slept in the hollow of an old tree. Kevin loved animals, but had no wish for contact with other people.

Lower down the mountain was a farm, which had a large herd of cattle. Each morning the farmer and his herdsman let the cattle out of their pen to graze on the mountain grass. One particular cow, who had an independent spirit, used to break away from the herd and walk up the mountain to Kevin's lake. Kevin was delighted to see the cow, and shared his herbs with her. In the evening the cow descended the mountain, and rejoined the herd just in time to return to the pen.

When the herdsman milked the cows at night, they found that this cow gave only cream – in the same quantity as the other cows gave milk. After some days the herdsman reported this to the farmer, saying that the cow must have found some exceptionally rich pasture. The farmer ordered the herdsman to watch the cow, to discover the pasture. The following day the herdsman followed the cow up the mountain to Kevin's lake.

The herdsman was astonished to see Kevin feeding herbs to the cow, and the cow licking Kevin's face in gratitude. The herdsman ran down the mountain, and told the whole neighborhood about Kevin.

THE BOAR

To Kevin's annoyance people now visited him, seeking his blessing. They said to him: "If you can turn a cow's milk into cream, you can turn my poverty into wealth." Kevin had no wish to make people rich, but he could not refuse to bless them. Finally he became so irritated by the interruptions that one night he left the mountain. He walked for many days until he reached a remote valley. There he built himself a hut and a chapel.

One day a wild boar came running through the woods, panting with exhaustion, and hid in Kevin's chapel. A few moments later a cruel huntsman called Brandub, notorious for killing both animals and humans merely for pleasure, arrived with a pack of snarling hounds. The hounds went up to the entrance of the chapel, but refused to go in, falling silent and bowing their heads. Brandub was on the point of yelling at the hounds, accusing them of cowardice, when he saw Kevin standing under a tree. Birds were perched on Kevin's arms, and were flying around his head, singing with joy. As Brandub stared at Kevin, a breeze arose, and the rustling of the leaves on the tree became a chorus accompanying the birds' song.

The cruel huntsman was filled with fear, and fell off his horse onto the ground. Then he crawled to Kevin, and begged his blessing. From that day onward Brandub never again killed either people or animals, and lived instead on wild herbs.

THE BLACKBIRD

He devoted himself to prayer and studying the Bible; and as he read, he would rest his arm on the window-sill of his hut, with his open palm turned upward. One day, when he was utterly engrossed in a particular passage of the Bible, a blackbird landed on his arm, thinking it was a branch. The bird looked at Kevin's palm, and decided it would make a good place to build a nest. It collected twigs and leaves, and within a short time had made a beautiful home.

Kevin now looked up from his book, and saw what was happening. He was filled with such love for the bird that he did not move. He watched the bird lay eggs and hatch them; and he remained in that position until the young birds could fly.

St. Kevin preferred the company of animals, whom he loved, to the presence of his fellow man.

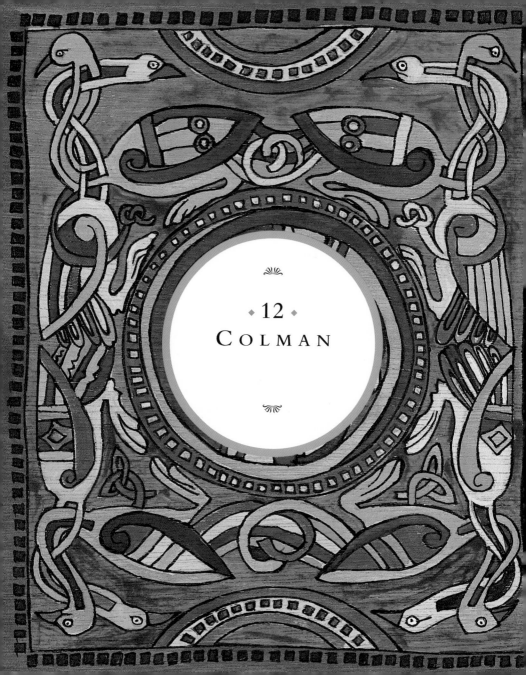

· 12 ·

COLMAN

THE MOUSE, THE ROOSTER, AND THE FLY

Colman wished to imitate the life of Jesus Christ in the wilderness. So he lived in a remote cave, and had no possessions – apart from his Bible. However, he had three small companions: a mouse, a rooster, and a fly.

The mouse used to wake Colman in the middle of the night by gnawing at Colman's bedclothes, and nibbling Colman's ear. Colman would then rise up and pray, and then go back to bed. The rooster used to wake Colman at dawn by crowing. Even when Colman was utterly exhausted from his long night vigils, the rooster kept crowing until he had actually risen – to save Colman from the sin of sloth.

But the fly's service was most remarkable. When Colman sat down to read the Bible, the fly used to walk down the page at precisely the same pace as Colman read the lines. And if Colman looked up from the page to reflect on what he had read, the fly stayed at the line – so when Colman continued reading, he could find his place at once.

At length these three creatures died, so Colman lost their loyal service and companionship. His heart was heavy with sorrow, so he wrote to his spiritual friend, Columba, abbot of Iona. Columba replied: "To you the rooster, the mouse, and the fly were as precious as the richest jewels; so rejoice in the fact that God has taken those jewels for himself."

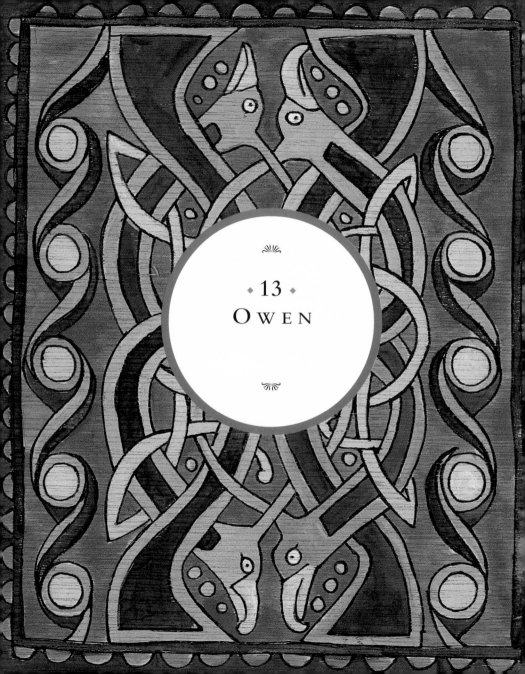

13

OWEN

Some years after Iltut's death, a miller in Wales wanted his son Owen to be a priest. So he saved up the profits from his mill, and sent his son to the school which Iltut had founded. Owen learned to read the Bible and also how to lead worship. After five years Owen was ordained, and returned to his village as a priest.

Owen wished to remain poor and celibate so that he could devote himself wholly to his priestly work. But while Owen had been away an older priest had taken charge of the village church; and Owen was shocked to discover that this priest had three women living with him, and that he lent money to the poor at extortionate rates of interest. Deciding that he could not work under such a wicked man, he began to serve the animals instead.

At night he slept in his father's mill, and in the morning he went out into the fields to talk to the sheep and cattle. He always had with him a large Bible, from which he would read to the animals; and at night he put the Bible under his head as a pillow.

At first the villagers thought Owen was mad. They laughed and jeered at him during the day, and at night they were afraid to go near him, for fear that he might attack them. But soon they noticed how much the sheep and cattle loved him, gathering round and listening to his gentle voice.

The old priest was so busy making money and enjoying himself that he had no time to teach the people. So two young men, hungry for true spiritual food, went out one day to join the animals. Impressed with Owen's words, the next day they invited their friends. Soon almost everyone in the village went into the fields to hear Owen preach – even on Sundays. So the village church was empty.

Eventually the corrupt priest died, and the people invited Owen to replace him. From that moment on the people never killed an animal for meat; they only took wool from the sheep and milk from the cows. They said that, since these animals had taught them to respect Owen's madness, they must respect the animals.

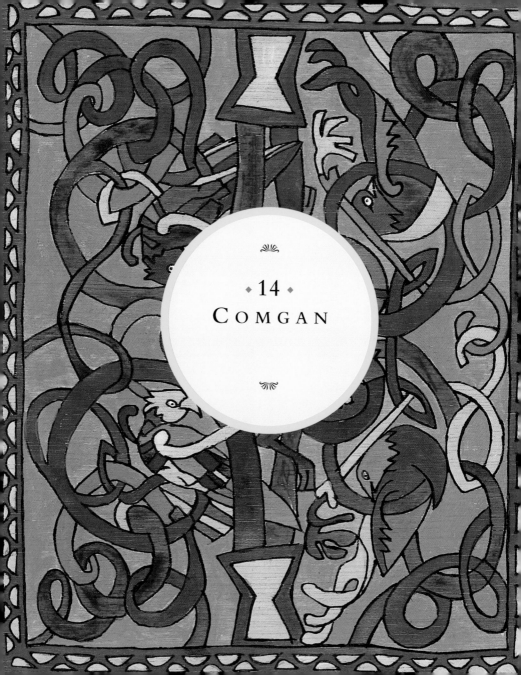

· 14 ·
COMGAN

THE DRUNKARD

Comgan was a wandering preacher in the west of Ireland. One day he saw a woman sitting outside a hovel, quietly weeping. He asked the woman what was wrong. The women explained that she had five children, and her husband was a drunkard. So he was spending all their money on drink, while the children dressed in rags and were hungry.

Comgan told the woman to borrow a cat, and keep in her hovel that night. Then, when dusk fell, Comgan went to the local tavern, and found her husband. He befriended the husband, chatting to him on all sorts of subjects. The man was impressed with Comgan's knowledge, saying to himself: "This wandering preacher has clearly been well educated."

When the man was so drunk he could hardly speak, Comgan said: "Do you know, if you carry on drinking like this, you will turn into a mouse." The man believed Comgan, and became extremely frightened. Comgan then led the man home. As the man opened the door of his hovel, he saw a cat on the table. "Get that cat out of here," he shouted, "or it'll eat me up." The cat fell out of the open door.

The man never touched drink again. Soon he was providing ample food and clothing for his family, and the following year he built them a pleasant cottage.

SEVENTEEN HORSES

Comgan arrived in a village when the local priest had just died. The priest had owned seventeen horses, but had not made a will. So the people of the village were arguing about who should have the priest's horses.

Comgan said: "I shall show you how to find the right person to be your new priest – and at the same time resolve your argument. Let the seventeen horses be divided in the following way. The sexton should have half the horses, the beadle a third, and the choirmaster a ninth. The person who can work out how to do this should be your priest."

The sexton, the beadle, and the choirmaster went in search of the person who could work out how to divide seventeen horses according to Comgan's formula. Lots of people tried, making calculations on their fingers, but concluded that it was impossible.

Then they met a young man, who said: "I shall give you my horse, which will bring the number to eighteen. Then the sexton can have nine horses, which is a half; the beadle can have six horses, which is a third; and the choirmaster can have two horses, which is a ninth. That makes seventeen. There is one horse left over – mine – which you can return to me."

The people then asked the young man to be their priest. They sent him to the local bishop to be trained and ordained. He returned and served them for many decades.

Comgan met a farmer who grew the finest soft fruits in western Ireland. But he had the two laziest sons in the region. They spent all day drinking and chatting with their friends, and never helped their father. The old man said to Comgan: "When I am dead, weeds will destroy my fruit bushes, and my sons will starve."

Comgan said to the two sons: "I have heard on good authority that there is treasure in the field where the fruit bushes grow. It is enough to feed and clothe you for the rest of your lives."

It was now September. The two brothers went to the field, and began searching for the treasure. They dug round every fruit bush, working from dawn until dusk in the hope of finding a casket of gold. By March they had dug half the field, and found nothing. "Keep digging," said Comgan; "I promise that if you do not find treasure by July, I will share half of my income with you. But if you find treasure, you must share half with the poor."

So the two brothers continued to dig, turning over the earth so that not a single weed survived. In July Comgan came to the field, and exclaimed: "I see you have found the treasure." "Where?" the brothers asked. "Look at the bushes," Comgan said; "they are heavy with luscious fruit."

From then onward the two brothers worked hard in the field. Each year they sold half the crop, and gave the rest to the poor. And, as Comgan had said, they had enough to feed and clothe themselves for the rest of their lives.

SHARING JEWELS

Comgan heard about a miser who owned a fabulous collection of jewels. The miser kept the jewels in a safe.

Comgan called on the miser, and said: "I hear you have a fabulous collection of jewels. Would you allow me to see them?" The miser replied: "It would be a pleasure. I haven't looked at them myself for many years, so I too shall enjoy seeing them."

The rich man opened the safe, took out a gold box and carefully placed the box on a table. He unlocked the box, and lifted the lid. Both Comgan and the miser stared with open mouths at the diamonds, rubies, emeralds, and sapphires which it contained. The miser dipped his hand in the box, and let the precious stones run through his fingers. Then after a few minutes he closed the box, and returned it to the safe.

"Thank you for giving me those jewels," Comgan said. The miser replied: "I haven't given them to you; they belong to me." Comgan said: "I have had as much pleasure as you from looking at them. So there is no difference between us – except that you have the expense and anxiety of buying and looking after them."

That day the miser gave away one jewel to every household in the town. There were just enough – with one left over for himself.

JUST THIEVES

A young thief, who was extremely successful at his wicked occupation, came one day to Comgan and confessed that his conscience was troubled. He expected Comgan to order him to desist from thieving at once. But to his surprise Comgan said: "I want you to find other young men,

and teach them to steal as successfully as you. Steal only from the rich, and give to the poor – keeping enough to feed and clothe yourselves."

The young thief did as Comgan proposed, gathering a small army of other young men. They began to steal gold and silver from all the castles and mansions in the region, giving what they had stolen to the poor. They were so skilled at thieving that they were never caught.

Finally in despair the rich people came to see Comgan, and pleaded: "Go and speak to these young thieves and urge them to stop. You are the only person they respect." Comgan answered: "I shall tell these thieves to stop at once – if you promise to use your wealth for the good of all."

By this means the region enjoyed a period of justice and honesty, such that it had never known before.

THE GRIEVING WIDOW

An old couple were admired by everyone in their village for the happiness of their marriage. They never quarreled, and were always loving and affectionate toward each other. Eventually the husband died, and the wife was overcome with grief. Her children and her neighbors tried to console her, but to no avail. Weeks and months passed, and still the old woman was grieving and inconsolable; tears of grief rolled down her cheeks from morning till night.

Comgan heard about her. He asked one of his wealthy friends to lend him a ring with a precious jewel set in it. He took it to the old woman, and said to her: "I want you to find a family which has no sorrows, and give that family this ring."

The woman set off in search of a family with no sorrows. She visited every home in the region and talked to every family. Finally she returned home, and gave the ring back to Comgan. Her grief had gone.

The Celtic parables are filled with divine meaning.

BIBLIOGRAPHY

This is a list of primary sources concerning Celtic Christianity.

Anderson, A.O. and M.O., *Adomnan's Life of St. Columba*, London, 1961.

Bieler, L., *The Patrician Texts in the Book of Armagh*, Dublin, 1979.

Carmichael, A., *Carmina Gadelica*, 2 vols, Edinburgh, 1928.

Clough, S.D.P., *A Gaelic Anthology*, Dublin, 1987.

Colgrave, R., *Two Lives of St. Cuthbert*, Cambridge, 1940.

Doble, G.H., *Lives of the Welsh Saints*, Cardiff, 1971.

Flower, R.E.W., *Poems and Translations*, London, 1931.

Forbes, A.P., *Lives of St. Ninian and St. Kentigern*, Edinburgh, 1874.

Graves, A.P., *A Celtic Psaltery*, London, 1917.

Greene, D. and O'Connor, F., *A Golden Treasury of Irish Poetry 600 to 1200 AD*, London, 1967.

Hull, E., *The Poem-Book of the Gael*, London, 1912.

Hyde, D., *The Religious Songs of Connacht*, 2 vols, Dublin, 1906.

Jackson, K., *Studies in Early Celtic Poetry*, Cambridge, 1935.

McLean, G.R.D., *Poems of the Western Highlanders*, London, 1961.

Metcalfe, W.M., *Lives of Scottish Saints*, 2 vols, Paisley, 1899.

Meyer, K., *Selections from Ancient Irish Poetry*, London, 1911.

Murphy, G., *Early Irish Lyrics*, Oxford, 1956.

O'Donoghue, D., *St. Brendan the Voyager*, Dublin, 1895.

Rees, W.J., *Lives of the Cambro British Saints*, Llandovery, 1853.

Sharp, E., *Lyra Celtica*, Edinburgh, 1896.

Stevens, J., *Bede's Ecclesiastical History of the English Nation*, London, 1910.

Stokes, W., *Lives of Saints from the Book of Lismore*, Oxford, 1890.

Webb, J.F., *Lives of the Saints*, London, 1965.